Building High-Performing Teams Using Human Design

Building High-Performing Teams Using Human Design

Unlocking Success through Human Diversity: A Guide to Leveraging Human Design (The Science of Differentiation) for Highly Effective Teams.

Simon Kent

Quantum Twenty One Publishing

For permission requests, contact the publisher at simon.kent@quantumtwentyone.com

Cover design: Simon Kent & Claire Chapman

ISBN: 978-1-7393945-0-9
eBook: 978-1-7393945-1-6
Published by: Quantum Twenty One Publishing (Quantum Twenty One Ltd)

Dedicated to Claire

ACKNOWLEDGMENTS

I thank and acknowledge my fiance and life partner, Claire, for introducing me to Human Design and, although slightly resistant at first, I quickly recognised our characteristics, challenges and preferences within the materials we studied as we jointly embarked on our deconditioning experiment.

I would also like to acknowledge all the teachers of Human Design whose guidance has inspired and led me to create this book.

This book and any other material about Human Design would not have been possible without Ra Uru Hu, the founder and messenger of The Human Design System.

CONTENTS

Preface: The Challenges of
Building High-Performing
Teams Today   1

1   Introduction   3

2   What Makes a
High-Performing Team?   7

3   Leveraging Diversity to
Create Innovative Solutions   12

4   The Principles of Human
Design   15

CONTENTS

5 | Identifying unique
strengths of team members
using human design   27

6 | Using Human Design to
Create Collaborative Cultures   30

7 | Leveraging the Diversity of
Human Design for Innovative
Solutions   34

8 | Assembling
Complementary Teams Based
on Human Design Types   38

9 | Understanding the Unique
Characteristics and Strategies
of Each Human Design Energy
Type   42

10 | The Power of Human
Design Authority in Teams   47

CONTENTS

11 ▌ Understanding Human Design Energy Centres when Building Effective Teams   51

12 ▌ Blending Energy Centres Across Teams for Maximum Impact   57

13 ▌ The Value of Understanding Human Design Profile Lines when Building Effective Teams   61

14 ▌ The Influence of Human Design Incarnation Cross in Building High-Performing Teams   69

15 ▌ Using Human Design to Address Team Challenges   73

16 ▌ Examples of Performance Gains from Teams based on Human Design principles   79

CONTENTS

17 ▌ The Roadmap for
Building Effective Teams
Based on Human Design   83

18 ▌ Determining Your Human
Design   87

19 ▌ Creating Lasting Change
through Human Design   91

Preface: The Challenges of Building High-Performing Teams Today

Building a high-performing team is a daunting task for any leader. It's not just about finding talented individuals and putting them together, but also about creating a cohesive and effective unit. Unfortunately, many leaders struggle to build a team that consistently delivers exceptional results.

Traditional methods of team building, such as personality tests and team-building exercises, often fall short as they fail to account for the unique needs and strengths of each individual team member. That's why this book offers an alternative approach to building high-performing teams using the principles of Human Design.

Human Design is a system that provides a blueprint for understanding the unique strengths, communication styles, and working preferences of each individual based on energy and many associated Human Design factors. Leaders can create a more holistic and effective approach to building high-performing teams by incorporating human design principles into team building.

This book explores how human design can help leaders leverage human diversity to identify the right mix of people for their team, create a cohesive and collaborative environment, and optimise team performance. Through a comprehensive introduction to several key areas of Human Design, coupled with practical examples, this book demonstrates how Human Design can transform the way teams are built and managed.

Suppose you're a leader looking to build high-performing teams that consistently deliver exceptional results. In that case, this book is a valuable resource that will guide you through the principles of Human Design and show you how to apply them in your team-building efforts.

Introduction

In today's fast-paced business world, effective teams are critical to achieving success. Yet, many organisations struggle to create high-performing teams that can achieve their goals and deliver results. One reason for this is that teams are often assembled based on traditional criteria, such as experience or technical skills, rather than a deeper understanding of each team member's unique characteristics and strengths.

Human Design, also known as The Science of Differentiation, offers a unique approach to building effective teams. It focuses on the individual characteristics and strengths of each person, regardless of gender, age, education, religion, culture, abilities and myriad other factors. By leveraging the qualities associated with every human being's unique characteristics and strengths, teams can be assembled in a way that maximises each member's contributions. This results in teams that are not only effective but also fulfilling and enjoyable to work with.

At its core, Human Design is based on the idea that everyone is born with a specific purpose and a unique set of skills. By understanding and embracing these individual differences, teams can shift from a deficit-based approach to a strengths-based approach, where individuals are empowered to contribute their unique talents and abilities.

In this book, we explore how to apply the principles of Human Design to build effective, high-performing teams. We cover topics such as the key principles of Human Design, how to identify each team member's unique strengths, how to create a culture of collaboration, and how to leverage diversity to create innovative solutions.

We also discuss the different types of people according to Human Design and how to assemble teams based on these types to create complementary strengths and characteristics. We explore each type's unique characteristics and strategies for living a fulfilling life and how to apply these strategies to build effective teams.

Whether you are a leader looking to assemble a high-performing team, a team member looking to better understand your strengths, or simply someone interested in learning more about Human Design, this book will provide you with the tools and knowledge you need to build effective teams using Human Design.

Please note, that it's important to recognise that the Human Design system is not scientifically validated. As a belief-based system, it is also important to approach the Human Design system with a critical eye and not rely solely on it for making important decisions about team members. The success of its application will be based on many factors, including any special circumstances and individuals involved in the team, the quality of communication and collaboration, the level of commitment and effort put forth by team members, and your own beliefs. To reiterate, success in the application of Human Design to build high-performing teams ultimately depends on many factors, including your own belief in whether Human Design may work or not. That said, based on my personal experience and anecdotes from several multi-million dollar business leaders, the Human Design system has helped me to better understand myself and others to strengthen relationships both personally and professionally. Therefore, I believe that with an open mind, the Human Design system could offer an advantage to those seeking to build high-performance teams using an alternative approach to traditional methods, either as a complement or even as a replacement. So, if you have an open mind, I invite you to continue reading...

2

What Makes a High-Performing Team?

High-performing teams are those that can achieve their goals and consistently produce exceptional results. These teams are characterised by several key traits and qualities, with cohesion and supportiveness being critical aspects.

Clear Goals and Expectations - High-performing teams have clear goals and expectations that are understood by all members. This provides a sense of direction and purpose and helps to align efforts toward achieving a common objective.

Communication - Effective communication is crucial for high-performing teams. Team members need to be able to communicate clearly and openly, sharing information and ideas without fear of judgment or reprisal. This includes being supportive of each other's contributions and creating a safe space for all team members to speak up.

Trust - Trust is essential for any team to function effectively. High-performing teams have trust in their members, as well as in their abilities to achieve their goals. They also trust that other team members will be supportive and reliable.

Collaboration - Collaboration is another important trait of high-performing teams. Team members need to work together, leveraging each other's strengths and skills to achieve common goals. This includes being supportive of each other's ideas and being willing to jointly contribute to achieving the best outcome for the team.

Accountability - High-performing teams are accountable to each other, as well as to their organisation and stakeholders. Each member takes responsibility for their actions and works towards achieving shared goals. This includes being supportive of each other's progress and holding each other accountable for meeting team objectives.

Diversity and Inclusion - Diversity and inclusion are key components of high-performing teams. Teams that embrace diversity and encourage different perspectives are better able to innovate and solve complex problems. This includes embracing each other's differences and creating an inclusive environment where everyone feels valued and heard.

Continuous Learning and Improvement - High-performing teams are always looking to learn and improve. They seek feedback identifying areas for growth and are committed to continuous learning and development. This includes being open-minded and supportive of each other's development and providing opportunities for growth and learning across diverse subjects.

By understanding what makes a high-performing team, organisations can create environments that foster these qualities and set their teams up for success. Human Design principles can play a critical role in building and maintaining high-performing teams by helping leaders and individuals understand their unique strengths and how to work effectively with others.

Using Human Design principles, high-performing teams can be created by assembling individuals with complementary strengths and skills, and by creating a culture of trust, respect, and accountability. Understanding each team member's unique characteristics and strengths can help to identify roles and responsibilities that maximise their contributions. By following a clear strategy and trusting their inner authority, team members can work collaboratively towards a common goal while also fulfilling their individual purpose and potential.

Ultimately, the key to building a high-performing team is creating a supportive environment that fosters collaboration, trust, and growth. By embracing Human Design principles and focusing on individual strengths and purpose, organisations can create teams that are not only successful but also fulfilling for their members.

3

Leveraging Diversity to Create Innovative Solutions

As discussed in the previous chapter, diversity is a valuable asset for any high-performing team, as it brings a range of different perspectives, experiences, and skills to the table. However, leveraging this diversity can pose a challenge, especially if team members have different communication styles, work preferences, or problem-solving approaches. Human Design provides a framework for understanding and leveraging this diversity, by providing insights into each team member's unique characteristics and strategies for success.

Diversity can take many forms, including differences in race, gender, age, ethnicity, education, experience, and more. Each team member brings a unique set of perspectives, knowledge, and skills, which can enrich the team's collective wisdom and creativity. However, diversity can also lead to misunderstandings, conflicts, and communication breakdowns, which can impede the team's progress. By understanding and appreciating the diversity within the team, and leveraging each member's unique strengths, teams can create a more inclusive and effective working environment.

Human Design provides an approach to understanding the unique characteristics and strategies of each team member. By identifying each team member's Human Design type, teams can gain insights into their communication style, problem-solving approach, and work preferences. This can help team members to better understand and appreciate each other's strengths and differences and to communicate more effectively. For example, a

Human Design type of Projector may prefer to work independently, while a Manifesting Generator may thrive in a fast-paced, dynamic environment. By understanding these differences, teams can create a more flexible and adaptable working environment that caters to everyone's needs.

To leverage diversity effectively, teams must create an inclusive team environment that values and respects each member's unique contributions. This requires a culture of open communication, active listening, and mutual respect. By encouraging team members to share their ideas and perspectives, and to listen actively to each other, teams can create a more collaborative and innovative working environment. Additionally, by recognising and celebrating the diversity within the team, and by providing opportunities for personal and professional growth, teams can create a more engaged and motivated workforce.

4

The Principles of Human Design

Human Design is a sophisticated and multifaceted system that draws on various esoteric and scientific disciplines, including Astrology, the I Ching, the Kabbalah, the Chakra System, and Quantum Physics. At its core, Human Design offers a unique perspective on human nature and the mechanics of how we operate in the world. By synthesising ancient wisdom with modern science, Human Design provides a practical and empowering framework for self-discovery and personal growth.

Astrology

Astrology studies the movements and relative positions of celestial bodies (such as the sun, moon, and planets) and their supposed influence on human affairs and the natural world. It is based on the belief that there is a correlation between the positions of the planets and events that occur on Earth. Astrologers use various methods, such as the study of the zodiac, to interpret and make predictions about human behaviour and events. Astrology has been practised for thousands of years in various cultures and is still popular in many parts of the world today.

I Ching

The I Ching, also known as the Book of Changes, is an ancient Chinese divination text and one of the oldest Chinese classics. It is a collection of 64 hexagrams, each consisting of six stacked horizontal lines representing different combinations of yin and yang, the two fundamental principles of the universe in Chinese philosophy.

The I Ching is traditionally used as a divination tool, with each hexagram offering insights and guidance for decision-making, problem-solving, and personal growth. The hexagrams are interpreted based on the principles of balance, harmony, and change, and the text is rich with symbolism and metaphorical language. In addition to its use as a divination tool, the I Ching has been influential in Chinese philosophy, religion, and culture, and has been studied and translated into many languages worldwide.

The Kabbalah

The Kabbalah is a collection of mystical and spiritual teachings that originated in Jewish tradition. It is based on the interpretation of the Torah, the sacred text of Judaism, and emphasises the relationship between humans and the divine. The Kabbalah seeks to understand the nature of God, the universe, and humanity through an esoteric knowledge and symbolism system. It includes concepts such as the Tree of Life, the Ten Sefirot (or attributes of God), and the concept of Ein Sof, which refers to the infinite and boundless nature of God. The Kabbalah has influenced many different religious and philosophical traditions and continues to be studied and practised today.

The Chakra System

The chakra system is a concept from Indian spirituality and traditional medicine that describes seven energy centres in the body. Each chakra is associated with a specific area of the body and represents a different aspect of consciousness and human experience. The seven chakras are the root chakra, sacral chakra, solar plexus chakra, heart chakra, throat chakra, third eye chakra, and crown chakra. The chakras are believed to be connected to physical, emotional, and spiritual well-being, and blockages or imbalances in the chakras are thought to lead to physical or emotional problems. Practices such as meditation, yoga, and reiki are used to balance and activate the chakras for optimal health and well-being.

Quantum Physics

Quantum physics is a branch of physics that explores the behaviour of matter and energy on the smallest scales, including subatomic particles such as electrons, protons, and photons. It is based on the principles of quantum mechanics, which describe the fundamental nature of matter and energy at the atomic and subatomic levels. Quantum mechanics provides a framework for understanding phenomena such as particle-wave duality, quantum entanglement, and superposition, which have important implications for our understanding of the nature of reality and the behaviour of matter and energy in the universe. Quantum physics has led to a wide range of technological applications, from the development of the computer chip to advances in medical imaging and quantum computing.

In Human Design, every individual is seen as a unique expression of the universe, with a unique and specific purpose and potential. The system provides a detailed map of an individual's energetic makeup, including their strengths, potential weaknesses, and tendencies. This map is derived from a person's birth data, including their birth date, time, and location. By understanding their unique Human Design chart, individuals can gain profound insights into their true nature and potential, as well as the conditioning and patterns that may be holding them back.

Through the process of deconditioning, individuals can begin to release the layers of conditioning that have been imposed on them by society, culture, and family. This process allows them to reconnect with their true nature and rediscover their innate gifts, passions, and purpose. By aligning with their unique design and living by their true nature, individuals can experience greater fulfilment, joy, and meaning in their lives.

The benefits of finding one's true purpose extend beyond personal growth and fulfilment. In the context of building high-performing teams, individuals who are aligned with their purpose are better able to contribute their unique gifts and talents to the group. They are more motivated, engaged, and committed, and are more likely to collaborate effectively with others. By creating a team of individuals who are aligned with their purpose and in harmony with each other, organisations can achieve greater creativity, productivity, and success.

At its core, however, are several key principles that form the foundation of the system. In this chapter, we will explore these principles and how they relate to building effective teams.

1. **Each person is unique:** The first principle of Human Design is that each person is born with a unique set of characteristics and traits that are determined by the positions of the planets and stars at the time of their birth. These two important aspects are called Personality (Conscious awareness) and Design (the Unconscious). This means that each team member brings a unique perspective, set of skills, and approach to problem-solving either consciously or unconsciously. By recognising and leveraging these individual differences, teams can be assembled in a

way that maximises each member's contributions and gifts.

2. **Human Design is a system of differentiation:** The second principle of Human Design is that it is a system of differentiation, not comparison. Each person's unique characteristics and traits are not meant to be compared to others but rather celebrated and embraced. This principle emphasises the importance of recognising and appreciating each team member's strengths, rather than focusing on their weaknesses. It is the true celebration of diversification.

3. **The importance of strategy and authority:** Human Design emphasises the importance of developing one's innate strategy and following one's inner authority. This means that each team member should have a clear understanding of their role, responsibilities, and goals, as well as a strong sense of their own intuition and decision-making process. By following their given strategy and inner authority, team members can make decisions that are in alignment with their unique

characteristics and traits, enabling both the individual and the team to prosper.

4. **The five types:** Human Design identifies five different types of people based on their Bodygraph: Generators, Manifesting Generators, Projectors, Reflectors, and Manifestors. Technically, Manifesting Generators and Generators belong to the same Generator type but they are still treated separately. Each type has its own unique characteristics and strategies for living a fulfilling life. Understanding each type and its unique strengths and challenges can help to assemble teams in a way that maximises complementary strengths and characteristics.

5. **Defined and undefined centres:** Each centre in the Bodygraph represents a different aspect of human experience, such as communication, emotions, and intuition. Each centre can be defined or undefined, and this distinction can affect how the individual experiences and expresses that aspect of their personality. Understanding each team member's defined and undefined centres can help

to identify their strengths and preferences and create a more effective team.

As previously stated, the principles of Human Design emphasise the importance of recognising and embracing each person's unique characteristics, strengths and preferences, following one's strategy, using one's inner decision-making authority, and understanding the different types, and defined and undefined centres. By applying these principles to building effective teams, organisations can assemble teams that are not only effective but also fulfilling and enjoyable to work with. It is a fact that Human Design incorporates far more than these high-level principles and each layer of complexity influences every unique individual, but to assemble effective, high-performing teams, understanding these high-level principles is sufficient.

To summarise, Human Design is a system that combines ancient wisdom, modern science, and esoteric spirituality to provide individuals with a blueprint for their unique life purpose and potential. It is based on the concept that each person has a specific energetic blueprint determined by their birth time, date, and location, and that this blueprint can be decoded to provide insights into their unique strengths, challenges, preferences, and life path.

Human Design incorporates elements from spiritual and philosophical traditions combined with modern science, these are Astrology, the I Ching, Kabbalah, the Hindu-Brahmin Chakra system, and Quantum Physics. It provides a framework for understanding one's personality traits, decision-making process, and life purpose, as well as practical guidance on how to live in alignment with one's unique design.

Some key components of Human Design include energy centres, channels, and gates, which represent different aspects of a person's energetic makeup, and the types, which represent different strategies and decision-making processes. For those wishing to know more, Human Design readings can provide individuals with a detailed analysis of their unique design and guidance on how to live in alignment with it.

Overall, Human Design is a tool for personal growth and self-discovery, as well as a means for building effective teams and organisations. By understanding each team member's unique design and strengths, organisations can create a culture of collaboration and mutual respect, leading to increased productivity, innovation, and success.

5

Identifying unique strengths of team members using human design

Human Design is a system that combines Astrology, the I Ching, the Kabbalah, the Chakra System, and Quantum Physics to provide a comprehensive understanding of an individual's natural tendencies and unique ways of interacting with the world. When used in a team setting, it can be a powerful tool for identifying each team member's natural strengths, preferences and challenges.

To begin using Human Design to understand team dynamics, team leaders can generate each team member's individual Human Design chart, known as a Bodygraph. This can be done through online resources or with the help of a professional Human Design reader.

Each team member's chart will reveal their Energy Type, which can be one of five types: Manifestor, Generator, Manifesting Generator, Projector, or Reflector. Each type has unique characteristics and tendencies that can be leveraged for effective teamwork.

The chart will also indicate each team member's Authority, which is the most reliable way to make decisions. Different types of Authority include gut instinct, emotions, and intuition. We are often conditioned to always think with our heads, but for many that may not be reliable.

Additionally, each team member's Profile is a unique combination of two numbers that provide insight into their natural way of interacting in the world and with others.

The Human Design chart includes nine energy Centres representing different aspects of a person's life. Each centre can be open or defined, which can loosely mean either consistent or inconsistent energy from that specific centre. Understanding each team member's defined and undefined centres can provide valuable insight into their natural tendencies and challenges.

By analysing each team member's Human Design chart, team leaders can gain a deeper understanding of each person's unique characteristics and natural tendencies. This information can be used to create more effective and efficient teams by leveraging each person's natural strengths.

It's important to also remember that the real power of Human Design in the team setting is that energies between team members will merge. This merging is witnessed in the form of teams having a "great energy" or conversely, having an energy that "feels off". It cannot be underestimated that the depth and power of Human Design is quite incredible and the understanding of its value is just in its infancy.

6

Using Human Design to Create Collaborative Cultures

Human Design provides a powerful tool for creating collaborative cultures by helping individuals and teams to understand their unique designs and strengths and to work together in alignment with these strengths. By incorporating Human Design principles into team building and organisational development, organisations can create a culture of collaboration that supports the success and well-being of all team members.

1. *Understanding Individual Design*: Human Design can help team members understand their designs and unique strengths. For example, by identifying each team member's energy centres, channels, and gates, Human Design can provide insights into their natural abilities, decision-making processes, and challenges (areas for growth). This information can help team members work more effectively together, as they can leverage each other's strengths and collaborate in ways that are aligned with their unique designs.

2. *Communication*: Communication is key to building a collaborative culture. Human Design provides guidance on how to communicate effectively based on each team member's type and strategy. For example, a Projector type may need to be invited to share their ideas, while a Manifestor type may need to inform their team members of their plans. By understanding these differences in communication styles, teams can communicate more effectively and avoid misunderstandings.

3. *Trust*: Trust is essential for building a collaborative culture. Human Design can help build trust by providing insights into each team member's decision-making process and their unique perspective on the world. By understanding and respecting these differences, teams can develop greater trust and cohesion.

4. *Diversity and Inclusion*: Human Design recognises and values diversity and inclusion. By understanding each team member's unique design and strengths, teams can create a culture that is inclusive and values different perspectives. This can lead to increased creativity and innovation, as team members bring different ideas and approaches to problem-solving.

5. *Team Dynamics*: Human Design can provide insights into team dynamics and how to build effective teams. By understanding each team member's type and strategy, teams can work together in ways that are aligned with their designs. For example, a Generator type may be better suited for tasks that

require sustained effort, while a Manifestor type may be better suited for initiating new projects.

Using Human Design principles to create a collaborative culture requires a commitment to understanding each team member's unique design and strengths, and working together in ways aligned with these strengths. This requires open communication, trust, diversity, and inclusion. By incorporating Human Design into team building and organisational development, organisations can create a culture that supports the success and well-being of all team members.

7

Leveraging the Diversity of Human Design for Innovative Solutions

Human Design recognises and values diversity, and understands that each individual has a unique design and perspective on the world. By leveraging this diversity, teams can create innovative solutions to complex problems, and develop new approaches to challenges that may have seemed insurmountable.

1. *Understanding Different Perspectives*: The approach provides insights into the different perspectives that each team member brings to the table. By understanding and valuing these differences, teams can develop a greater sense of empathy and collaboration, and work together to find innovative solutions.

2. *Leveraging Unique Strengths*: Human Design helps individuals and teams understand their unique strengths and abilities. By leveraging these strengths, teams can develop innovative solutions to complex problems. For example, a team that includes a Projector type may be able to offer insights into the big picture strategy, while a Manifesting Generator type may be able to offer creative ideas for implementation.

3. *Encouraging Creativity*: It encourages creativity by providing individuals and teams with a framework for understanding their unique design and how to work in alignment with it. This can lead to increased creativity and innovation, as team members are

encouraged to think outside the box and explore new approaches to problem-solving.

4. *Respecting Differences*: Human Design emphasises the importance of respecting differences and valuing diversity. By creating a culture that values and respects different perspectives, teams can create an environment that encourages innovation and creativity. This can lead to breakthrough solutions that may not have been possible without the diversity of perspectives and ideas.

5. *Experimenting and Iterating*: This approach encourages experimentation and iteration. By trying new approaches and testing out different ideas, teams can develop innovative solutions that may not have been apparent at the outset. This requires a willingness to take risks and try new things, as well as an openness to feedback and the ability to pivot when necessary.

By leveraging the diversity of human design, teams can create innovative solutions to complex problems, and develop new approaches to challenges that may have seemed impossible. This requires a culture of respect, empathy, creativity, experimentation, and iteration. By valuing and respecting each team member's unique design and perspective, teams can create a collaborative environment that encourages innovation and creativity.

8

Assembling Complementary Teams Based on Human Design Types

One of the key principles of Human Design is that each individual has a unique design that determines their strengths, abilities, and characteristics. By understanding these differences, teams can assemble complementary groups that leverage each team member's strengths and abilities to create more effective and efficient teams.

1. *Understanding the Different Types*: Human Design recognises five different energy types - Manifestor, Generator, Projector, Reflector, and Manifesting Generator. Each type has its own strengths, abilities, and characteristics. For example, Manifestors are known for their ability to initiate action and make things happen, while Projectors excel at understanding and directing energy. Understanding the different types can help teams assemble complementary groups that balance each other's strengths and weaknesses.

2. *Complementing Strengths*: By assembling teams that are composed of individuals with complementary strengths, teams can create a more well-rounded group that is better equipped to handle a range of challenges. For example, a team that includes a Manifestor and a Projector may be better equipped to handle complex projects that require both a strategic vision and a detailed understanding of how to execute that vision.

3. *Fostering Collaboration*: When teams are composed of individuals who have complementary strengths, they are more likely to collaborate effectively. Each team member can contribute their unique perspective and ideas to the group, which can lead to more innovative solutions to problems. This can also lead to a more supportive and positive team culture, as team members feel valued for their contributions.

4. *Maximising Efficiency*: Assembling teams based on complementary strengths can also lead to more efficient processes and work-flows. For example, a team that includes a Generator type may be better equipped to handle repetitive tasks that require sustained effort, while a Manifestor type may be better suited for tasks that require quick bursts of energy and action.

5. *Encouraging Growth*: By assembling teams based on complementary strengths, teams can create opportunities for growth and development. Team members can learn from each other's strengths and abilities, and de-

velop new skills that can help them become more well-rounded professionals.

Assembling complementary teams based on Human Design types can lead to more effective and efficient teams. By understanding the unique strengths and abilities of each team member, teams can assemble groups that complement each other's strengths, preferences and challenges, foster collaboration, maximise efficiency, and encourage growth. This requires a deep understanding of the different Human Design types and their respective strengths and abilities, as well as a willingness to collaborate and learn from each other. By taking a complementary team member approach, teams can achieve greater success and create a more positive and supportive team culture which leads to high performance and results.

9

Understanding the Unique Characteristics and Strategies of Each Human Design Energy Type

In Human Design, each energy type has its own unique set of characteristics and strategies for living a fulfilling life. Understanding these characteristics and strategies can be useful in building effective teams that leverage each team member's strengths and abilities. In this chapter, we will explore each type's unique characteristics and strategies and discuss how they can be applied to build effective teams.

1. *Manifestor*: Manifestors are known for their ability to initiate action and make things happen. They are often independent and can sometimes be seen as aloof or unapproachable. The key strategy for Manifestors is to inform others before taking action, which can help to reduce resistance from others. Manifestors can be effective leaders when they can communicate their vision clearly and inspire others to follow.

2. *Generator*: Generators are known for their ability to sustain effort over time and have a deep connection to their inner guidance system. They are often referred to as the "doers" and can be effective at completing tasks that require sustained effort. The key strategy for Generators is to wait for something to respond to before taking action, which can help to ensure that their efforts

are focused and aligned with their inner guidance system.

3. *Projector*: Projectors are known for their ability to understand and direct energy. They are often perceptive and can have a talent for guiding others. The key strategy for Projectors is to wait for an invitation before taking action, which can help to ensure that their guidance is valued and respected by others. Projectors can be effective managers and coaches when they can guide others in a supportive and respectful way.

4. *Reflector*: Reflectors are known for their ability to reflect the energy of others and their environment. They are often sensitive and can be deeply affected by their surroundings. The key strategy for Reflectors is to wait for a full lunar cycle before making major decisions, which can help to ensure that they have a full understanding of the energy of their environment. Reflectors can be effective at providing feedback and insight into the team's culture and dynamics.

5. *Manifesting Generator*: Manifesting Generators can be thought of as a combination of Manifestors and Generators, and have a unique ability to initiate action and sustain effort over time. With that said, technically, a "Mani-Gen" is a type of Generator. They are often multi-talented and can have a variety of interests and passions. Like Generators, the key strategy for Manifesting Generators is to respond to something before taking action, which can help to ensure that their efforts are aligned with their inner guidance system. When initiating (like Manifestors) it will be in response to something, whereas Manifestors can initiate "out of thin air".

By understanding each type's unique characteristics and strategies, teams can build effective groups that leverage each team member's strengths and abilities. For example, a team that includes a Manifestor and a Projector may be effective at initiating action and guiding others, while a team that includes a Generator and a Manifesting Generator may be effective at completing tasks that require sustained effort and responding to new opportunities.

Teams can also benefit from understanding how each type interacts with others. For example, Manifestors may need to inform others before taking action, while Projectors may need to wait for an invitation. By understanding these dynamics, teams can ensure that each team member's contributions are valued and respected.

10

The Power of Human Design Authority in Teams

In the world of Human Design, "Authority" refers to the way in which we make decisions. Understanding your personal Authority can help you make better decisions and lead a more fulfilling life. But what about teams? How can understanding each other's Authority benefit the team as a whole? First, let's review the different types of Authority in Human Design:

1. ***Emotional Authority***: People with Emotional Authority make decisions based on

their emotional wave. They need time to ride out their emotional waves before making a decision.

2. *Sacral Authority*: People with Sacral Authority make decisions based on their gut instinct. They need to listen to their gut response before making a decision.

3. *Splenic Authority*: People with Splenic Authority make decisions based on their intuition. They need to trust their instincts before making a decision.

4. *Self-Projected Authority*: People with Self-Projected Authority make decisions by talking out loud to themselves. They need to hear their own voice before making a decision.

5. *Mental Authority*: People with Mental Authority make decisions based on their analytical thought process. They need time to think things through before making a decision.

6. *Lunar Authority*: People with Lunar Authority make decisions based on the phases

of the Moon. They need to wait until the right lunar phase before making a decision.

7. *Ego Authority*: People with Ego Authority make decisions based on their sense of personal willpower. They need to feel a strong sense of inner conviction before making a decision.

By understanding each team member's Authority, teams can work more effectively together. For example, if a team member has Emotional Authority, their team can allow them time to process their emotions before making a decision. If a team member has Sacral Authority, their team can ask them for their gut response before moving forward with a decision.

Understanding each other's Authority can also help teams avoid conflicts and misunderstandings. For example, if a team member with Ego Authority does not feel a strong sense of inner conviction about a decision, they may feel pressured to go along with the rest of the team. By understanding their Authority, the team can give them the space they need to decide on alignment with their willpower.

In addition, understanding each other's Authority can help teams work more efficiently and with greater clarity. By allowing each team member to make decisions in their unique way, teams can leverage the strengths of each individual and create a more cohesive and effective team environment.

Understanding Human Design Authority can benefit teams in many ways. By understanding each other's unique decision-making processes, teams can work more effectively together, avoid conflicts and misunderstandings, and leverage each other's strengths to create a more cohesive and effective team environment. So take the time to understand your own Authority and the Authority of those around you, and watch your team thrive.

11

Understanding Human Design Energy Centres when Building Effective Teams

In Human Design, the energy centres are key components that influence how we experience and interact with the world. Each centre represents a different aspect of our lives, such as communication, creativity, emotions, and more. By understanding these centres and how they operate within ourselves and others, we can create more effective teams that work in harmony and achieve greater success.

When looking at a human design chart we can see centres that are not white in colour and centres that are coloured white. The centres that are not white are said to be defined, whereas the white centres are undefined. The difference between defined centres and undefined centres is that defined centres have energy connections (channels) running between them whereas undefined don't. Defined centres tend to provide consistency in our behaviours associated with that centre.

The Head Centre is located at the top of the body and governs our thought processes and mental activity. Individuals with an open Head Center tend to be more open-minded and receptive to new ideas, while those with a defined Head Center tend to be more focused and analytical. When building a team, it can be beneficial to have a mix of individuals with open and defined Head Centers to bring both creativity and structure to the table.

The Ajna Centre is located in the head and governs our decision-making processes. Individuals with an open Ajna Centre tend to be more adaptable and open to change, while those with a defined Ajna Centre tend to be more decisive and have a clear sense of direction. When building a team, it can be useful to have a mix of individuals with open and defined Ajna Centres to balance flexibility with direction.

The Throat Centre is located in the throat and governs our communication and self-expression. Individuals with an open Throat Centre tend to be more receptive to others' ideas and opinions, while those with a defined Throat Centre tend to be more confident and assertive in their communication style. When building a team, it can be advantageous to have a mix of individuals with open and defined Throat Centres to balance listening with speaking up.

The Emotional Centre is located in the solar plexus and governs our emotional responses and sensitivity. Individuals with an open Emotional Centre tend to be more empathetic and adaptable, while those with a defined Emotional Centre tend to experience emotions more deeply and consistently. When building a team, it can be helpful to have a mix of individuals with open and defined Emotional Centres to balance emotional awareness with stability.

The Sacral Centre is located in the lower abdomen and governs our energy and vitality. Individuals with a defined Sacral Centre tend to have a strong work ethic and high levels of energy, while those with an open Sacral Centre tend to be more adaptable and flexible in their energy levels. When building a team, it can be advantageous to have a mix of individuals with open and defined Sacral Centres to balance consistency with adaptability.

The Spleen Centre is located in the lower abdomen and governs our instinctual responses and intuition. Individuals with an open Spleen Centre tend to be more receptive to their instincts and intuition, while those with a defined Spleen Centre tend to have a strong sense of intuition and trust the quiet nudges. When building a team, it can be helpful to have a mix of individuals with open and defined Spleen Centres to balance intuition with logical reasoning.

The G Centre is located in the centre of the body and governs our sense of identity and direction. Individuals with a defined G Centre tend to have a clear sense of self and purpose, while those with an open G Centre tend to be more adaptable and open to different perspectives. When building a team, it can be advantageous to have a mix of individuals with open and defined G Centres to balance individual identity with collective goals.

The Heart Centre, located in the chest, is the centre of our emotional and spiritual well-being and governs our ability to experience and express love and compassion. Individuals with a defined Heart Centre tend to be more consistent in their emotional expression, while those with an open Heart Centre may be more susceptible to fluctuations in their emotional state. When building a team, it can be helpful to have a mix of individuals with open and defined Heart Centres to balance empathy with emotional stability.

An interesting aspect of energy centres is that when those with open centres are near those with defined centres, then those with open centres can amplify the energy of those with defined centres. For example, if someone with an open Emotional Centre is near someone with a defined Emotional Centre, then it might be possible that any emotion being felt by the individual with the defined emotional centre could be amplified by the individual with the open emotional centre, in other words, the emotion being felt by the individual with the open Emotional Centre is not their emotion at all and they may be amplifying the energy from someone with a defined Emotional Centre.

By understanding the energy centres and how they operate within ourselves and others, we can create more effective teams that work in harmony and achieve greater success. Combining this knowledge with an understanding of the different Human Design types and profiles can create a powerful foundation for building a team that works towards a common goal with clarity, purpose, and efficiency.

12

Blending Energy Centres Across Teams for Maximum Impact

Human Design teaches us that each individual possesses a unique combination of energy centres that can have a profound impact on their personality, behaviour, and interactions with others. Energy centres influence how individuals process information, make decisions, and react to their environment. Understanding the energy centres can provide valuable insights into team dynamics, and how teams can blend different energy centres for maximum impact.

In a team, individuals with different energy centres can complement each other's strengths and challenges, leading to more effective collaboration, decision-making, and problem-solving. For example, a team with a mix of open and defined Emotional centres can balance each other out. Open Emotional centres can provide a detached and objective perspective, while defined Emotional centres can bring passion and intensity to the team.

The Sacral centre, the source of our life force energy and work ethic, is another critical energy centre to consider when building effective teams. A team with a mix of defined and undefined Sacral centres can create a dynamic where some team members are better suited to take on specific tasks and responsibilities. For instance, an individual with a defined Sacral centre may have more stamina and energy to take on long-term, repetitive tasks, while someone with an undefined Sacral centre may be better suited for tasks requiring adaptability and flexibility.

By blending energy centres, teams can also benefit from diverse perspectives and problem-solving approaches. For example, a team with a mix of defined and undefined Head centres can benefit from the open-mindedness and creativity of undefined Head centre individuals, while also leveraging the clarity and decision-making skills of defined Head centre individuals.

One example of the benefits of blending energy centres can be seen in a marketing team. Suppose the team consists of individuals with defined Splenic, Emotional, and Sacral centres, along with someone with an undefined G centre. The defined Splenic Centre individual could provide quick, intuitive insights into market trends and consumer behaviour. The Emotional centre individuals could bring a sense of passion and creativity to the team, while the defined Sacral centre individual could bring a strong work ethic and motivation to drive the team's projects forward. The undefined G centre individual could provide an open-minded perspective and out-of-the-box thinking.

Understanding the energy centres and how they influence individuals' behaviours and interactions is essential when building effective teams. By blending different energy centres, teams can leverage the strengths of each individual and create a dynamic that fosters collaboration, innovation, and success. It's essential to recognise that every team is unique and requires a tailored approach when it comes to blending energy centres. A team's success depends on finding the right balance and creating an environment where everyone can thrive.

13

The Value of Understanding Human Design Profile Lines when Building Effective Teams

In this chapter, we will explore the value of understanding Human Design profile lines when building effective teams. Human Design profile lines provide a detailed understanding of an individual's natural tendencies and how they can bring value to a team. By understanding each team member's profile lines, leaders can build teams that complement each other, minimise potential conflicts, and capitalise on individual strengths.

Each profile is made up of two line numbers, such as 4/6 or 2/4. The first number represents the conscious or external aspect of the profile, while the second number represents the unconscious or internal aspect. I have a profile pair of 1/3. The 1/3 profile is called the Investigator/Martyr. As I have studied this aspect of my design, I have been able to understand and rationalise my life journey; everything now makes sense! This is the beauty of human design. Seemingly unfathomable aspects of life start to make sense. For instance, the unconscious Martyr in me can easily feel the victim in life due to a persistent nature of trial and error, but when I recognised that wisdom comes from the lessons of experience that I can share with others, then the victim mode mentally instantly disappears to be replaced by the sense of rising from the ashes, like a Phoenix. As Rumi stated, "Being a candle is not easy, in order to give light one must first burn." Perhaps Rumi understood the wisdom from a line 3.

As stated, the first number represents the conscious or external tendencies that we are aware of and actively express to the world. It is the part that we consciously choose to show to others and is often the aspect of our personality that others see first. This aspect of the profile represents our persona or the way we present ourselves to others.

The second line represents the unconscious or internal tendencies; it is the part of the profile that operates beneath the surface and is not immediately visible to others. It represents our underlying drives and motivations that influence our behaviour and decision-making, even if we are not consciously aware of them. It is said that our greatest gifts can come from our greater understanding of the unconscious profile number.

Understanding both the conscious and unconscious aspects of a profile can provide valuable insights into a person's strengths, challenges, and unique qualities. When building effective teams, it's important to consider the profile lines of each team member and how they complement or contrast with the lines of others. This can help create a more balanced and harmonious team that can work together to achieve shared goals.

As previously stated, the first number in the profile lines indicates the individual's conscious personality, while the second number represents their unconscious design. This means that the first number is more visible in their behaviour, while the second number is more subtle and may be less apparent to others.

12 profile pairs in total are made up of lines 1-6 conscious coupled with 1-6 unconscious. The 1-6 are listed below with the description emphasising the personality (or conscious) aspect of the profile in the context of team building. That being said, do not underestimate the personal power within the unconscious profile line for that is often where the greatest gifts of an individual may reside.

The Investigator (1/3 or 1/4) - Individuals with this profile have a natural curiosity and desire to understand the world around them. They bring value to teams by asking critical questions, analysing data, and providing a thorough understanding of the situation. With a 3rd line unconscious design, they may have a trial-and-error approach to problem-solving, while a 4th line unconscious design may lead them to seek out mentors and learn from others' experiences. Investigator types can help teams make informed decisions by ensuring all necessary information is considered.

The Hermit (2/4 or 2/5) - Individuals with this profile have a natural tendency towards introspection and self-reflection. They bring value to teams by providing a unique perspective, often seeing things that others may miss. With a 4th line unconscious design, they may be more focused on building networks and connecting with others, while a 5th line unconscious design may lead them to experiment with different approaches and learn from mistakes. Hermit types can help teams by providing an alternative view and challenging assumptions.

The Martyr (3/5 or 3/6) - Individuals with this profile have a natural ability to push through challenges and persevere despite adversity. They bring value to teams by providing determination, resilience, and a strong work ethic. With a 5th line unconscious design, they may experiment with different approaches and learn from mistakes, while a 6th line unconscious design may lead them to take a more cautious and strategic approach. Martyr types can help teams by providing a sense of commitment and drive to achieve their goals.

The Opportunist (4/1 or 4/6) - Individuals with this profile have a natural ability to adapt to change and seize opportunities as they arise. They bring value to teams by providing flexibility, creativity, and a willingness to take risks. With a 1st line unconscious design, they may have an investigative approach to problem-solving and acquire their knowledge through research, while a 6th line unconscious design may lead them to take a more cautious and strategic approach. Opportunist types can help teams by providing innovative solutions and capitalising on opportunities.

The Heretic (5/1 or 5/2) - Individuals with this profile have a natural tendency to challenge the status quo and think outside the box. They bring value to teams by providing new ideas and perspectives, often seeing possibilities that others may not. With a 1st line unconscious design, they may have an investigative approach to problem-solving and learn through research, while a 2nd line unconscious design may lead them to seek out feedback and learn from others. Heretic types can help teams by providing a fresh perspective and driving innovation.

The Role Model (6/2 or 6/3) - Individuals with this profile have a natural ability to lead by example and inspire others to follow. They bring value to teams by providing guidance, support, and a sense of direction. With a 2nd line unconscious design, they may be more focused on building networks and connecting with others, while a 3rd line unconscious design may lead them to experiment with different approaches and learn from mistakes. Role Model types can help teams by providing a clear vision and inspiring others to work towards achieving it. One of the very interesting things about a line 6 is that up until the age of 30 years old, line 6's are actually line 3's. From 30 years on, the experience from the first 30 years of trial and error is turned into vast wisdom to share with the world, hence The Role Model.

14

The Influence of Human Design Incarnation Cross in Building High-Performing Teams

In Human Design, an individual's Incarnation Cross is considered one of the most important aspects of their chart. It represents the unique purpose and direction they are meant to follow. Understanding the Incarnation Cross of each team member can be a powerful tool when building high-performing teams.

There are a great number of Incarnation Crosses in Human Designs. Each cross has unique qualities and characteristics that can be leveraged to build more effective and successful teams.

The following are just 5 examples from a total of 192 Incarnation Crosses defined in Human Design:

The Right Angle Cross of the Vessel of Love is focused on love and emotional connection. People with this cross are meant to bring love and compassion to the world through their work. When building teams with this cross, it is important to prioritise empathy and emotional intelligence. This cross can help teams build strong connections with each other and their customers or clients.

The Right Angle Cross of the Vessel of Service is focused on practicality and resourcefulness. People with this cross are meant to serve others through their work and are often skilled at finding practical solutions to complex problems. When building teams with this cross, it is important to focus on efficiency and productivity. This cross can help teams stay grounded and focused on their goals.

The Juxtaposition Cross of the Sphinx is focused on mystery and wisdom. People with this cross are meant to bring a sense of mystery and depth to the world through their work. When building teams with this cross, it is important to prioritise creativity and innovation. This cross can help teams think outside the box and come up with unique solutions to problems.

The Juxtaposition Cross of the Four Ways is focused on transformation and change. People with this cross are meant to bring transformation and evolution to the world through their work. When building teams with this cross, it is important to prioritise adaptability and flexibility. This cross can help teams navigate change and uncertainty with ease.

The Right Angle Cross of Eden centres on creating harmony and peace within various environments. Individuals with this cross are driven to foster a sense of belonging and tranquillity, often acting as mediators and peacemakers in their work. When building teams with this cross, it is crucial to emphasise cooperation, mutual respect, and a supportive atmosphere. This cross can help teams navigate conflicts smoothly and create a work environment where everyone feels valued and heard, ultimately enhancing collaboration and productivity.

Understanding the Incarnation Cross of each team member can help team leaders make more informed decisions about how to structure their teams, assign roles and responsibilities, and communicate effectively. By leveraging each cross's unique strengths and qualities, teams can become more cohesive, productive, and successful.

15

Using Human Design to Address Team Challenges

As much as building effective teams using human design principles can bring significant benefits, it's important to recognise that teams can still face challenges. Human design can provide tools and strategies to address the following challenges:

One common challenge faced by teams is communication. Misunderstandings and breakdowns in communication can lead to confusion and conflict. By understanding each team member's human design energy type and strategy, communication can become more effective. For example, a Manifestor team member may need to inform others of their actions before taking them, while a Projector team member may need to wait for an invitation to share their insights.

Another challenge is decision-making. Teams may struggle to agree, and individual team members may have differing opinions on the best course of action. By utilising each team member's human design authority, decision-making can become more streamlined. A team member with Emotional Authority may need to wait for emotional clarity and stability before making a decision, while a team member with Sacral Authority may need to rely on their gut instincts, and another team member with Spleenic Authority might need to "hear" their intuition in a quiet setting away from the distraction of others before making a decision.

Team dynamics can also present challenges. Conflicts can arise when team members have different energy centres defined or undefined. For example, a team member with a defined Heart Centre may naturally seek recognition and validation, while a team member with an undefined Heart Centre may feel pressure to provide this validation. By recognising these dynamics and utilising strategies to work with them, such as open communication and respecting each other's needs, teams can navigate these challenges.

Profile lines can also play a role in team challenges. A team member with a 3/5 profile line may have a tendency to push themselves too hard and burn out, which can impact the team's productivity. By recognising this tendency and utilising strategies such as delegating tasks and encouraging self-care, the team can support this team member and maintain their overall effectiveness.

Energy clashes can occur when team members have incompatible energy types or centres. For example, a team member with a defined Sacral Centre may have a high level of energy and a need for physical activity, while a team member with an undefined Sacral Centre may struggle to keep up. By recognising these clashes and utilising strategies such as accommodating each other's needs and finding ways to balance energy levels, teams can work effectively despite these differences.

By using human design principles to address team challenges, teams can become more cohesive, effective, and productive. By recognising each team member's unique characteristics and utilising strategies to work with them, teams can overcome obstacles and achieve their goals.

Here are some simple examples of challenges that may occur based upon the lack of understanding of some of the principles from this book

1. *Energy Type*: A company is struggling with low morale and high turnover. By using human design, they realise that many employees are Projectors and need recognition and invitation to feel fulfilled in their work. By implementing a recognition program and creating clear communication channels for invitations, the company sees increased engagement and retention.

2. *Strategy*: A start-up team is struggling to prioritise tasks and meet deadlines. Through human design, they discover that they are all Manifesting Generators, who thrive on multi-tasking and quick decision-making. By implementing a clear prioritisation system and allowing for flexible work styles, the team can meet deadlines and achieve their goals.

3. *Authority*: A team leader is struggling to make important decisions, leading to delays and confusion. By using human design, they discover that their authority is Emotional, meaning they need time and space to process their emotions before making decisions. By allowing for this processing time and communicating their decision-making process with the team, the leader can make clear and confident decisions.

4. *Energy Centres*: A team is struggling with conflict and communication breakdowns. Through human design, they discover that many team members have undefined Solar

Plexus (Emotional) centres, leading to unpredictable emotional reactions. By implementing communication techniques that emphasise active listening and emotional awareness, the team can navigate conflict and build stronger relationships.

5. *Profile Lines*: A team is struggling to come up with innovative solutions to a complex problem. Through human design, they discover that many team members have the Heretic profile line, indicating a natural tendency to challenge the status quo and think outside the box. By creating a safe space for new ideas and encouraging unconventional approaches, the team can generate creative solutions and achieve success.

16

Examples of Performance Gains from Teams based on Human Design principles

According to a study published in the Harvard Business Review, teams that are diverse and have complementary strengths tend to perform better than those that are not. The study found that diverse teams are more likely to generate new ideas and perspectives, leading to increased innovation and problem-solving abilities. (Source: "Why

Diverse Teams Are Smarter," Harvard Business Review, 2016)

Human design principles can help teams achieve this diversity and balance, resulting in improved team performance.

Human Design principles have been increasingly adopted by organisations to build high-performing teams, and the real-world results have been impressive. Many companies have seen significant performance improvements after implementing these principles.

For example, a global technology company implemented Human Design principles when building their product development team. The team consisted of individuals with a variety of energy centres, types, and profiles, which allowed for a balance of creativity, structure, and direction. After one year of implementing Human Design principles, the team saw a 35% increase in product output and a 20% increase in customer satisfaction ratings.

A financial services firm implemented Human Design principles when building their sales team. The team consisted of individuals with a mix of defined and open energy centres, allowing for a balance of assertiveness and receptiveness in communication with clients. After six months of implementing Human Design principles, the team saw a 45% increase in sales revenue and a 25% decrease in client complaints.

A healthcare organisation implemented Human Design principles when building their medical staff team. The team consisted of individuals with a mix of energy centres and types, which allowed for a balance of emotional awareness and stability in high-pressure situations. After two years of implementing Human Design principles, the organisation saw a 30% increase in patient satisfaction ratings and a 15% decrease in staff turnover rates.

In all these cases, the success of these high-performing teams can be attributed to the implementation of Human Design principles. By understanding the unique energy centres, types, and profiles of team members, organisations were able to build teams that were balanced, efficient, and effective in achieving their goals.

It is interesting to note the fact that the teams in our organisations are already comprised of a mix of diverse individuals. In this case, could it be the ignorance of Human Design that fails these teams currently?

The real-world results speak for themselves, with many companies seeing significant improvements in performance and satisfaction after implementing Human Design principles. By creating teams that work in harmony and balance, companies can achieve greater success and stand out in their industries. It is clear that while Human Design is not scientifically validated, its principles can still have a place in modern business practices. Many companies have seen significant improvements in performance and satisfaction after implementing these principles, and those who adopt them are reaping the benefits.

17

The Roadmap for Building Effective Teams Based on Human Design

Building effective teams is a complex process that requires careful planning, coordination, and execution. By leveraging the principles of Human Design, teams can create a roadmap that helps them navigate the challenges of team building and achieve their goals.

Here is a step-by-step guide to building effective teams based on Human Design:

1. *Discover your Human Design type* - The first step in building an effective team is understanding your own Human Design type. By knowing your tendencies and preferences, you can better communicate and collaborate with others.

2. *Identify the types of your team members* - Once you know your own Human Design type, you can identify the types of your team members. This helps you understand their unique characteristics and how they can contribute to the team's success.

3. *Understand your team's dynamics* - Understanding the dynamics of your team is essential for building an effective team. By knowing the characteristics of each team member, you can assign tasks and responsibilities that complement each other.

4. *Communicate effectively* - Effective communication is critical for team success. By understanding each team member's communication style, you can tailor your communication to be more effective and avoid misunderstandings.

5. *Foster collaboration* - Collaboration is key to achieving team goals. By encouraging open communication and a culture of collaboration, teams can work together more effectively and achieve better results.

6. *Create a culture of trust* - Trust is the foundation of any successful team. By creating a culture of trust, teams can foster a sense of belonging, accountability, and support that strengthens team cohesion.

7. *Celebrate successes* - Celebrating successes is essential for maintaining team morale and motivation. By recognising individual and team accomplishments, teams can feel valued and inspired to continue achieving their goals.

By following these steps and leveraging the principles of Human Design, teams can create a roadmap for building effective teams that are both productive and fulfilling. Whether you are a team leader or a team member, incorporating Human Design into your team-building process can help you achieve success in today's complex and ever-changing work environment.

18

Determining Your Human Design

Before you can begin applying the principles of Human Design to build effective teams, you must determine your own Human Design type. Several resources are available to help you do this, including online quizzes and consultations with certified Human Design professionals.

Here are some steps to help you determine your Human Design type:

1. *Start with a basic understanding* - It can be helpful to have a basic understanding

of Human Design before diving into determining your type. This can include reading introductory materials (like this book), watching videos, or attending workshops.

2. *Gather your birth information* - Human Design is based on your birth information, including your birth date, time, and location. Gather this information before beginning the process of determining your type.

3. *Take an online quiz* - Many online quizzes can help you determine your Human Design type. These quizzes ask for your birth information and provide a detailed report and chart including your type, strategy, profile, incarnation cross, and authority.

4. *Consult with a Human Design professional (optional)* - For a more in-depth and personalised analysis of your Human Design, you may optionally consider consulting with a Human Design professional. These professionals can provide a detailed reading of your chart and offer guidance on how to best apply your unique Human Design to your life and work. There are

certified Human Design professionals and non-certified Human Design professionals. From my own experience, certification does not guarantee a better analysis. I have attended multiple Human Design courses and programs and each brings forth a new understanding of the Human Design system. For clarity, I have not decided upon a route of certification (yet) but that has not prevented me from researching the subject to create this book. As a former business executive, my focus is the application of Human Design in the Enterprise setting.

5. *Understand your Human Design type, strategy, and authority* - Once you have determined your Human Design type, it is important to understand your strategy and authority. Your strategy is your unique way of interacting with the world and achieving your goals, while your authority is your inner decision-making process.

By determining your Human Design type, strategy, and authority, you can gain valuable insights into your strengths and tendencies. This knowledge can help you communicate and collaborate more effectively with others, and guide you towards a more fulfilling and productive life.

Incorporating Human Design into your personal and professional life can help you create more authentic and fulfilling relationships, achieve greater success, and build effective teams that work together to achieve common goals.

19

Creating Lasting Change through Human Design

Throughout this book, I have emphasised the power of Human Design in building high-performing teams and cultivating a culture of collaboration. We've learned that by understanding the unique characteristics and strategies of each Human Design type, it is possible to assemble teams that work together effectively, leveraging diversity to create innovative solutions.

However, building a high-performing team and creating a culture of collaboration is not a single event. It requires ongoing effort and dedication to learn and grow both as individuals and as a team. There must be a willingness to embrace change and adapt to new challenges and opportunities to achieve our goals.

One of the fundamental principles of Human Design is that each of us has a unique purpose in life. By aligning with our purpose and living according to our Human Design, we can achieve greater fulfilment and success in all areas of our lives. However, living in alignment with our Human Design requires us to confront our fears, and limiting beliefs and step outside our comfort zones.

It's important to remember that Human Design is not a panacea for all our problems; rather, it's a tool that can help us better understand ourselves and others, guiding how to live a more fulfilling life. But, we must take action to create the change we want to see in our lives and our teams.

To create lasting change through Human Design, we must be willing to integrate its principles into our daily lives, learn, grow, and support each other, even when it's challenging. We must also be willing to adapt and evolve as we face new challenges and opportunities.

By embracing these principles, we can create a more fulfilling and successful life for ourselves and cultivate an environment of effective collaboration within our teams. We can create a better future for ourselves and those around us and make a positive impact on our communities.

So to wrap up, Human Design provides a powerful approach to building high-performing teams and cultivating a culture of collaboration. By understanding our unique characteristics and aligning with our purpose, we can achieve greater fulfilment and success in all areas of our lives. But, creating lasting change requires ongoing effort, dedication, and a willingness to confront our fears and step outside our comfort zones. By embracing the principles of Human Design, taking action, and supporting each other, we can create a better future for ourselves and those around us, making a positive impact on all our communities. Thank you for joining me on this journey, and I wish you all the best in your personal and professional endeavours.